$ENEFITS
Re-Imagined

Moving the Needle on Your Health-Care Costs

Troy Reichert, MBA

Benefits Re-Imagined: Moving the Needle on Your Health-Care Costs

© 2019 by W Troy Reichert
978-0-9843866-6-6

SEISMIC
PUBLISHING GROUP

Published by Seismic Publishing Group (seismicpg.com)

Printed in the United States of America

2 3 4 5 6 7 8 / 24 23 22 21 20

Table of Contents

Introduction

The Oxford dictionary defines freedom as "the power or right to act, speak, or think as one wants."[1] Our country is the land of the free and the home of the brave. But do you feel you have freedom in your health care? Do you have enough information to make good decisions about your medical care? Do you have any power to legitimately influence the costs of your medical insurance? If you and your employees feel trapped by steep deductibles, high co-insurance, and stiff co-pays, this book is for you. As a business owner or manager, once a year you consider the cost of health insurance, and you probably ask your broker about options. What is the usual answer? You can shop it, switch carriers, or change deductibles, co-pays, or co-insurance. But none of these choices help you or your employees afford the health insurance. You go through another renewal season, making some adjustments or concessions, but nothing really changes except now you're paying more in premiums. How would you like to see a menu of options that could move the needle on costs? How would you like to have input and controls that help you and your employees have affordable, quality health care and the freedom to choose? Would you like to have more choices in where you go and who you see for your medical care?

The rising costs of medical care and health insurance have become one of the hottest topics and most debated issues in recent years. According to the Centers for Medicare and Medicaid Services (CMS) website, health-care spending represented 18 percent of the gross domestic product in 2017.[2]

Almost every individual and family has seen and experienced the repercussions of these costs. From increased deductibles and out-of-pocket expenses to prescription costs and health-insurance premium increases, everyone is affected in some form or fashion.

Most people believe they have no control, no choice, and no power in this situation. "The costs are what they are" is the mentality. With tax incentives, preferred providers, and big insurance carriers controlling the market, many business owners and individuals think they are pawns in a game controlled by these corporations and *big money*.

If that describes your feelings, then this book is for you. It will outline the choices you have, the programs you can take advantage of, and the decisions you can make. One of the best ways to help people is to give them hope. The message from politicians and the news media is that the government is the only hope, that a one-payer system is the way to go.

The philosophy outlined in these pages does not agree with that option. There is a health-care system built. There are willing providers, hospitals, doctors, and other caregivers who offer meaningful services at fair prices. It's not about access to care; the problem is the hoops and processes we must go through to access and pay for that care. And too often these payments involve the pricing shell game played by the insurance carriers.

One of the most important takeaways from this book is that there is a vast difference between *health care* and *health insurance*. Too often these two concepts are used interchangeably. As you read this book, keep these two issues separated. Health care is how we look after our physical bodies and the means by which we get medical attention. Visiting a doctor, having a surgical procedure done, going to the pharmacist to get a prescription—these actions are all about health care. Health insurance is just that: insurance. This is a means by which many individuals pay for their medical care.

There are millions of people who get health care but do not have traditional health insurance. There are four primary categories of people who do not have traditional insurance.

1. Medicare: This is a government program for people age sixty-five or older, certain younger people with disabilities, and people with end-stage renal disease.[3] In 2018, there were approximately sixty million people covered by Medicare.[4]

2. Medicaid: This government program provides health coverage for some low-income people, families and children, pregnant women, the elderly, and people with disabilities.[5] As of February 2019, there were approximately seventy-two million people covered by this program.[6]

3. Medical cost-share programs: This program involves group members sharing one another's risk and costs. There is a basic monthly premium (very

low by most standards), and the group is notified when claims from individuals need to be paid.

Each member then helps pay for the claim expenses by donating to the cause or giving directly to the person who submitted the claim.

4. Uninsured: There were approximately 28.3 million uninsured individuals in 2018.[7]

In the US, approximately 162 million people do not have traditional health insurance.[8] This group represents 50 percent of the population as of June 2019.[9] Approximately 176.7 million people have traditional employer-based insurance or individual policies.[10]

The content of this book is primarily for those covered by employer-based health-insurance programs. However, many of the concepts are for anyone who cares about the true costs of their medical care.

Having choices and a willingness to pay for those choices is an integral part of our American way of life. When you purchase a vehicle, you can buy a new Fiat, Honda, Ford, Toyota, or Chevy for less than $18,000. But if you want to spend more, there are vehicles you can purchase that are well over $300,000, such as a Ferrari, Lamborghini, Aston Martin, Mercedes Benz, Bugatti, Bentley, or Rolls-Royce. And, certainly, there is every price point in between. As Americans, we place a high value on choices. Just consider how many choices we have at the supermarket for something as mundane as ketchup or mustard.

We have also been taught and conditioned to not think about cost when we are making health-care choices. Our doctor says we need an MRI and she tells us, without consideration of cost, where to go to get that done. In almost any major city in America, you can get an MRI done for as much as $4,000 or as little as $800. What is the difference between the two MRIs? Nothing! Just the price. It's really no different than one dealership charging more than another dealership, except you as the insurance buyer don't know there is a difference, as there's no method to shop or compare prices.

This book is about choices! It will teach you, your employees, and your family how to be wise consumers about the choices you have, the costs associated with those choices, and the options you have for your medical care and treatment.

How Did We Get Here?

A brief history of hospitals will give you some background and context of how our health-care system has evolved.

The modern system of health care has progressed significantly over the past hundred years. In the 1920s, hospitals were a place where the poor went to die. Society was surrounded by snake-oil salesmen and of potion pushers that were little more than placebos. Many hospitals were run by either the government or religious organizations. At the end of that decade, there was a transition in both mind-set and practice that caused more people to go to the hospitals for care.

During the Great Depression, both hospital administrators and citizens were faced with tough decisions about care, costs, and community access to medical treatment. On the cutting edge was Baylor University Hospital in Dallas, where the "Baylor Plan" was developed to help area citizens afford hospital care.[1] The concept was simple: allow a person or family to pay a little each month in exchange for medical care that may be needed in the future. This revolutionary concept was the first prepaid hospital insurance plan in the United States and the predecessor of Blue Cross.

As the country emerged from the Great Depression, hospitals and access to care expanded as a result of the Hill-Burton Act in 1946. This allowed more people to migrate to getting care within the hospital rather than at home. Advancements in technology and science turned hospitals from places to die to places where people were cured. Community hospitals grew substantially in the 1950s and 1960s with the influx of money from the federal government. Soon available patient beds outpaced the number of hospital stays, and the business of marketing hospital care was born.

There was another catalyst that catapulted health care to its next level and set the trajectory that became the employer-based health-care system we have today. During World War II, as the government rationed everything to support the war effort, employers had to find ways to compete and attract more workers. Fringe benefits became the avenue whereby employers attracted their workers, and offering medical benefits to employees became the norm. During the 1940s, less than 10 percent of the population had medical insurance through their employers. This grew to more than 60 percent by the mid-1950s and then more than 70 percent by the 1970s.[2]

Much like a concert venue or sporting event being a success or failure based on the number of people in the seats, hospitals are interested in "filling the beds." There is infrastructure, maintenance, employees, and fixed costs to keep hospitals open and ready to treat patients. Like any other business, bills need to be paid. Getting patients in the door became and continues to be a key concern. This plays out in new ways today as outpatient-care revenue begins to eclipse inpatient care.

Market pressures and creativity led to the development

of HMO and PPO networks. Contracted pricing and set fees helped control medical costs, and like any good business, hospitals needed a fee schedule, first developed in the 1950s. With the emergence of PPOs and contracted prices, discounts off the chargemasters became a place of negotiations. And that is when the games began. Through the structure of health insurance, employees were inadvertently taught that the price of their medical care was made up of the premiums paid plus the co-pays and co-insurance. We go to the doctor and pay $25 or $30 as the co-pay and we *think* that's all there is. However, few recognize that someone, somewhere, is actually paying the rest of the cost. That doctor's office bills the insurance company $135 or $150. Then based on the negotiated discount from the PPO network, that doctor is reimbursed for that claim. What we as consumers pay for our medical care is not the total cost.

If by now you feel confused, join the crowd. Our system is very convoluted in many respects. Even with the Affordable Care Act (ACA) and the price-transparency requirement that took effect in January 2019, many consumers cannot find the information to make an informed consumer decision. The 906-page H.R.3590 and the subsequent 27,000 pages of regulations have not made it any easier for consumers to understand. Yet getting a handle on the foundational principles of health insurance, health care, and provider pricing will help all of us become better consumers of our health care and medical insurance.

The true price of medical care is complex. There are many stakeholders in the system, from doctors and hospitals to the manufacturers of medical equipment and drugs. And the one player that sits in the middle of all of this, and as such controls the market, is the PPO. It's much like a teeter-totter, with providers on one side and patients on the other. The PPOs and HMOs sit in the middle, making money no matter which side goes up.

The point of this book is to give you—the business owner, manager, or administrator—and your employees information and ideas to:

1. Help understand the system
2. Gain insight about how to best play the game
3. Give ideas and alternatives so you, the consumer, have choices
4. Provide information so you can influence the costs

We live in a free-market economy. As consumers, we can buy the name brand and pay 10 to 30 percent more for the same commodity, or we can choose to buy the generic package. We can buy a car for $25,000 or $250,000. We have choices. The goal of this book is to make you aware of the choices you have. All you have to do is ask a few questions.

Market pressure and competition will dictate costs, but consumers have to know about the options in order to make choices. If consumers believe there is only one option, companies can charge whatever they want. And in the case of health care, consumers really don't understand *how* they pay for this care. Subsequently, they think they don't have any decision to make or that their choices don't matter anyway.

In some respects, it is a philosophical discussion. At the same time, it is an extremely costly one. We can have universal health care, and then no one will care or think about the cost. But that is the most expensive and costly system in the world. Free isn't really free, and it is certainly not good or excellent. When there is no incentive for the consumer or provider, everyone loses because there is:

- No motivation for excellence
- No reward for creativity
- No inducement to streamline
- No enticement to remove waste from the system
- No stimulus for innovation
- No consequence for inefficiency
- No repercussions for bad outcomes
- No penalty for terrible service
- No fallout for wrong decisions

Let's fix our system by educating the consumer and decision makers, providing price transparency and removing some of the factors that don't contribute to the overall well-being of the system or to the health of your employees.

Show Me the Money

Where do we start? How about with the money? An understanding of where the money is and where the money goes will help lay the foundation. In the current political realm, heath care is *all* about the money. There is a huge amount spent on health care, and many people, many companies, want a piece of that money, want to control more of that money, and want to influence how *you* spend that money. "U.S. health care spending grew 3.9 percent in 2017, reaching $3.5 trillion or $10,739 per person. As a share of the nation's Gross Domestic Product, health spending accounted for 17.9 percent."[1] Just to put that into perspective, according to *Forbes*, The World's Largest Public Companies list, the top 50 companies annual revenue is $6.468 billion.[2] It would take the combined annual revenue of these fifty global companies 541 years to equal one year of the US health-care spending. That, my friend, is called *big money*. That is why politicians argue over it and want to control it. I don't know about you, but it's hard for me to comprehend that figure.

To get a visual on the size of the health-care spending in

America, consider a football field. A regulation football field, including the end zones, is approximately 1.3 acres. If you stacked hundred-dollar bills seven feet high, it would take a little less than *two* football fields to hold a trillion dollars.[3] It would take almost *six* football fields stacked seven feet high with hundred-dollar bills to hold 3.5 trillion dollars. That's a lot of money!

Let's make it more real and talk about you and me. How can we understand this? How can we make new decisions? What can we do about the impact on *our* wallets and bank accounts? According to the Kaiser Family Foundation, employer-sponsored health-plan premiums for family coverage increased to $19,616 in 2018.[4] In 1999, those costs were $5,791. The employee-only rate has increased 314 percent since then, while the family premiums have increased 339 percent.[5] Since 2008, average family premiums have increased 55 percent, twice as fast as workers' earnings (26 percent) and three times as fast as inflation (17 percent).[6] We're all feeling the pinch of higher premium costs, deductibles, co-pays, and co-insurance.

Each of us is pulling more money out of our paychecks, pockets, and bank accounts for health insurance and ultimately our health care. The good news is, in any free-market economy, market pressure *will* create new opportunities. And even with the plethora of information we have access to today because of the internet, most of us don't know we have options, where to find those options, and how we can access them. Your reading this book is the first step on the journey to finding some of these opportunities. And hopefully you'll learn how you can find other choices, when you should ask questions, and where you can find additional information.

Now, let's get down to where the rubber meets the road. You're a CFO, employer, human-resources director, or manager tasked with overseeing the medical plan for your employees. Over the years, you've had **B**lue Cross (Blue Shield or Anthem in some states), **U**nitedHealthcare, **C**igna, **A**etna, or other similar national providers as your health insurance. In the insurance world, we affectionately call this group the **BUCA**s. Of the 5.6 million businesses in the US, the majority are small businesses with fewer than five hundred employees. Employers with fewer than a hundred employees represent 98 percent of those businesses.[7] This market is served by the BUCAs, which offer canned plans with fixed premiums. We have been taught and conditioned over the years to make sure we go to an in-network provider. The PPO networks have become the driving force and controlling element in the current health-care-delivery system. There are stiff penalties in terms of co-pays and co-insurance for not going to a network provider.

However, this is the root of our problems. The PPO system is a philosophy. This philosophy controls the hospitals, providers, and patients. In fact, it limits the choices for you and me. The PPO has become the middleman in this system, and while the middleman once provided value, now it controls the system. The middleman has become the gatekeeper. The gatekeeper controls access. The gatekeeper controls pricing. The gatekeeper becomes the dictator in our present health-care system.

The gatekeeper always adds costs to the system. Every person, department, and vendor in the delivery system adds cost. If we can remove some of the steps, remove some of the departments that don't add value or make the system more efficient, we can reduce costs. Although the health-care system is very complex, when you identify the participants in the system, realize the financial rewards and incentives, and know your choices, you can make new decisions and offer employees hope in this complex, vital, and important system.

Let me take you one step further into the morass of the health-care-delivery system and explore how the PPO system adds costs to the system. The BUCAs must have providers. Without the providers in network, the BUCAs have no value. The BUCAs must also offer the companies that purchase their health-care plans some kind of value. They have sold this value for years as their "discounts." BUCA provider A has this overall discount off billed charges. BUCA provider B has another discount off billed charges. And depending on the area of the country you live in, one BUCA PPO has a better discount than the others. But in some states, such as Alabama and South Carolina, Blue Cross seems to have a monopoly-like hold on the providers, and there seems to be relatively little competition or viable alternatives. But let's unpack this and understand what this really means.

Let's follow the money. And *this* is where the reality of the system will make you mad. This is where the curtain is pulled back and the wizard in the *Wizard of Oz* is exposed. Unfortunately, you as the buyer don't see this in the current purchasing model. These steps are behind the scenes, and you don't know how you can change the costs or the system.

But you are about to find out how you *can* change and take control of your part of this system. Knowledge is power, and you are about to pick up a very powerful piece of information. There is an incredibly intricate system by which the BUCAs contract with and set up their networks of providers. What follows is a simplified five-step process that will reveal how the prices are established and the network discounts are set up.

STEP ONE

A BUCA PPO network goes to a hospital facility in your area to negotiate the contract for the next two or three years. The current contract may say the hospital will bill this PPO 49 percent of the billed charges. You, the company, then get a discount of 51 percent off the billed charges. You may be wondering, *Who controls the charge amount?* I'm glad you asked, because that *is* the question to ask. Save the question, and I'll answer it in Step Five.

STEP TWO

The BUCA PPO network negotiates, pressures, threatens, incentivizes, and does whatever it can to get that hospital to give them *more* of a discount. To validate that this really happens, just do a quick Google search of the following and see what comes up on the first page:

- Blue Shield negotiations
- UnitedHealthcare negotiations
- Cigna negotiations
- Aetna negotiations
- Anthem negotiations

Every search will provide the same result: ABC facility speaks about negotiations with XYZ PPO. And most of it is not positive. These articles are about the tension between the gatekeeper and the providers.

STEP THREE

BUCA and the facility reach an agreement. Maybe the facility now agrees to a 51 percent discount of the billed charges. The BUCA PPO then goes to its clients (you and me) and says, "Hey, see how good we are? We've increased the discounts. We're fighting on your behalf." And in that statement, what is left unsaid? If you read between the lines, what is the message we hear? *Now I'm going to pay less. If Walmart reduces its prices, I'm going to pay less, right?* But the reality is, that's not what happens in the health-insurance world.

STEP FOUR

The BUCA then sets their plan rates. Do these prices *ever* go down because they've done such a great job negotiating on your behalf and thus reducing your costs? Are you kidding me? NO, the prices of the PPO plans don't go down.

STEP FIVE

ABC facility and their board of directors gets together to review their financials. In light of the new contracted discounts and agreements with the BUCAs, they realize they will not be as profitable. So, what do they do? They raise their prices. The chargemasters are the price listings from each facility they load into their computer system so they can charge each patient in a consistent manner. The hospital board approves changes and increases the chargemasters. To answer your previous question of who controls the charge amount, each hospital sets their retail price.

Do you see it? Did you get the math? If you're throwing things now or your blood pressure has gone up or your face is red, you get it! The philosophy is "I'll give you any discount you want up to ninety-nine percent as long as you let me set the retail." Certainly the health-care system has evolved. It didn't start out like this. But this is one of the reasons why health care has become *big* business and *big* money.

Who loses in this case? Not the hospital, as they have the power to increase their chargemasters. Not the PPO network, as they control the price you pay for their health plans. You do, your employees do, their families do—you all lose!

Who's to blame? Who is the bad guy in this situation? Well, there is plenty of blame to go around. I want to give you information so you can change your situation. If you want to read more about this in detail, check out the excellent article by Dave Chase in *Forbes*.[8]

You can also read more about the chargemasters and get more details on the hospital revenue cycle[9] online at Xtelligent Healthcare Media.

Now you know why you're so exasperated with health care and why your employees are fed up with the system. You know there is a problem. You know that businesses can't keep absorbing these price increases, and your employees can't take on the additional burden of higher premiums, co-pays, drug costs, and co-insurance.

Well, keep reading. While I don't promise to have the silver bullet, I believe that an informed person is an armed person. When you have better information, when you know some of the inside story, you can play the game more effectively and actually win. You can make new decisions that will give you more control.

"The U.S. federal government is on an unsustainable fiscal path.... The single thing that drives our unsustainability is health care spending."

—Federal Reserve Chairman, Jerome Powell, speaking to Congress on February 26, 2019.

Chapter 3

New Lenses, New Perspective

When you started to read this book, I'm sure you had questions. Internally, there may have been some frustration, maybe a lot. And like any respectable business leader, you are watching the money, watching the costs, and feel as though there are no options, no good choices. As you read the news, talk to others about the health-insurance conundrum, and maybe even discuss it with your broker or consultant, you will find that the following seem to be the only viable options:

1. Terminate your health plan
2. Absorb the costs
3. Pass the costs on to your employees
4. Raise the deductible, co-pays, and/or co-insurance

These are the options and alternatives we've been fed for the past ten years. You and I both know these are not good ones.

But there is another option! Walt Disney "saw" another option for family entertainment. Herb Kelleher "saw" another possibility for air travel when he drew his idea for Southwest

Airlines on a napkin. Bill Gates "saw" a new way to leverage the power of the computer, while IBM ignored his idea. Yes, there is another way to "see" your benefits. The answer is not a company, it is not another insurance carrier, and it is not another PPO network—it is a concept. It's an idea that has been around for a long time. But this concept has to be re-imagined today and applied to your situation.

Imagine if you could design a medical-benefits program that fit your company, your employees, and your budget.

Imagine if you could "see" all the costs, including claims and prescriptions, and better understand how these costs affect your medical plan.

Imagine if you could direct your employees and their families to certain doctors, facilities, surgical centers, and hospitals that would show you their prices so your plan members would know what the costs were up front.

Imagine if you could provide incentives that reward people for their behavior and choices.

Imagine if you could help your unhealthy people get the help and care they need while helping control plan costs.

Imagine if you could reduce the out-of-pocket costs for your employees and their families.

Imagine if you had providers who were your partners in helping your employees get or stay healthy.

Yes, imagine! But you don't have to just imagine this as if it were some movie that was only fiction and had no basis in reality, because that reality is available to you today. Contrast that with this story about Henry Ford. Early in Ford's manufacturing career, people asked him if he would consider offering other colors of his Model T. His response was, "You can have any color Ford you want, just so long as it is black." That is the exact response you get from the BUCAs. They offer you plain vanilla, no options, no control, no insight, and no help with managing your costs, claims, or plan.

When was the last time a BUCA sent you a report telling you what your top ten claims were?

When was the last time a BUCA sent you a report telling you how much you spent on prescriptions by generic, brand, and preferred?

When was the last time a BUCA sent you a report showing an analysis of costs by the age group of your members?

When was the last time a BUCA came and offered you some ideas on how to influence utilization or encourage members to consider costs when they chose providers or treatments?

Unless you're part of a large company employing more than five hundred employees, you may never have seen one of these reports. And if you have, how timely were they? There are carriers in my state who give companies some reports— three or four months after the claims occurred! So, if you had a large claim in September, you wouldn't see it in any report until January. Wow. I don't know about you, but what good is that? That's like hearing about the news three months later. Even during World War II, news got back to the United States faster than that. And we live in the digital age, where information is king and the speed of that information is crucial to everyday decisions. Amazon gets sales information instantly, but you and I can't get a medical claims report that is timely or relevant.

This is about to change. You have a choice. You have an opportunity. Imagine what decision you would make if you had timely information that could lower your medical-plan costs.

Imagine what decisions your employees would make if they had better information. The PPO model has trained people to stay in network. Although that is okay, there are so many more decision points they should consider when choosing a provider or electing a course of treatment.

What is the choice you have? What is the option? The answer is a simple solution: a self-funded medical plan. You may have heard this term or even had a self-funded medical plan before. Your experience may have been good, or it may have been bad. Before you discount this option, before you think you know what I'm talking about, read on and learn what this means today. And if you're an employer with less than fifty employees, read on as well, because there are options for you too.

Being self-funded may sound scary, expensive, and risky. Some people may have had a bad experience with this concept. I can assure you, your concerns and experiences are valid. If you didn't have a knowledgeable broker or consultant advising you and had a self-funded plan offered by one of the BUCAs, you may have had a bad experience. If you had a plan blow up because of shock claims, disreputable brokers or underwriters, or inappropriate plan design, you had an unfortunate experience. But the choices, controls, and programs available today can help you have a much better experience with self-funding. With updated research, the speed of information, and companies that have developed new solutions for medical care, the options are remarkable.

But let's start with the basics, and then we'll get into these controls and safeguards. Self-funded medical plans have been around for decades and are underwritten in a similar way as your current plan. A self-funded medical plan has ID cards and access to doctors, hospitals, surgeons, imaging centers, and pharmacies. There is a summary plan document just like your BUCA plan. There are customer-service people who help your employees when they have questions or problems. But that is where the similarities end. A self-funded plan offers information, controls, savings programs, and choices that the BUCA plan does not. What does it mean to go to a self-funded plan?

First, being self-funded means that you get rid of the BUCAs. I know, BUCAs offer self-funded options and they always tout their network and their discounts. But don't be fooled: that's the same system that has been offered over the past thirty years—the same system that has brought us to this point of frustration, higher costs, and no control. But is their solution really different? Is it different *enough*? Do they offer solutions for controlling costs or utilization? Do they offer ways to reduce claims? Do they even *care* about the claims bucket? Not really. A BUCA's perspective on the claims bucket is much like the government's perspective on its budgets: "It's a bucket of money that we get to spend, and it's a bad thing if we leave any money in that bucket, because next year they will think we don't need that amount of money." Do you see and hear the incentive? Their incentive is to have more money in the bucket *next* year. *Your* incentive is to have money left over in the bucket *this* year. They have no incentive to have money left in the bucket. As the business owner, manager, or HR leader, you want to control the amount of money spent in that bucket. Imagine if your office supplies, rent, or taxes went up by 8 or 10 percent each year. But we've been trained to think that kind of increase in health-insurance premiums is normal, expected, and acceptable.

Second, being self-funded means that you have more options. Thus, you and your HR department will need to be engaged at a new level. Someone will need to be monitoring how the plan is running, how claims are going, and the flow of money in and out of the spending bucket. And your employees will need to learn how their choices affect the plan and eventually their costs. Self-funding is not a "set it and forget it" plan like the BUCAs. How many CEOs or HR leaders consider their medical plans *after* the renewal? We all go through the renewal process complaining and wishing there were alternatives, but then we move on to other priorities until the next renewal season. This won't be how it is with a self-funded plan. You'll want to watch your medical spending as much as you watch your company's financial performance.

Finally, being self-funded doesn't mean you have no insurance. That's one of the biggest misconceptions. In the early days of self-funding, only the big companies were able to take advantage of this concept, and they probably started without insurance coverage. They had the cash flow and size to protect the plan. Over the past twenty years, insurance carriers such as American International Group, Swiss Re, Liberty Mutual, Sun Life Financial, Tokio Marine, National Union Fire, Munich RE, Berkshire Hathaway, and Voya Financial have developed new contracts that are appropriate for smaller employer groups. Because of this, self-funded medical plans are available to a much broader group of employers. Now self-funding is a viable option for thousands of small-businesses that make up such a huge segment of our economy.

So, if we don't get rid of insurance but we get rid of the BUCAs, how does this system work? Self-funded plans are designed and work very similarly to BUCA ones. In most plans, there is a network of doctors and providers. Like with BUCAs, self-funded plans have an ID card, prescription benefits, and pre-certification for certain medical procedures. There is a customer-service line for your members to call with questions or problems or for help on their Explanation of Benefits (EOB). On the surface, these self-funded plans look like and act like your fully insured plans. However, there is a completely new level of information and choices that you have. A self-funded medical plan offers the three Cs:

1. Choice
2. Control
3. Communication

First, you have many choices of how you design your benefits program. The sky is the limit on creativity. While each plan must comply with current federal regulations, there are numerous options. This can be likened to the difference between a Cessna 152 and a Gulfstream G600. Both are airplanes, they will get you somewhere faster than if you were to drive, but they are extremely different in how they get you to your destination and how fast you get there. The Gulfstream flies at 710 miles per hour and has a range of 7,400 miles.[1] The Cessna flies at 127 miles per hour and has a range of about 500 miles.[2] A BUCA plan is like a Cessna: you have very few controls, fewer indicators and instruments to help you, and even fewer options for customization. A self-funded plan is like the Gulfstream: there are so many more options, controls, and indicators to help you see what is going on. Both the BUCA plan and the self-funded plan will provide medical coverage for your employees, but the choices you have and the amount of money your company and employees spend out of pocket can be vastly different.

With choice also comes some new responsibilities. Your HR staff and your employees and their dependents will have to be re-educated. The PPOs have done a disservice, as too many people think the co-pay is all their doctor's appointment costs. In reality, the patient pays the co-pay but the doctor's office then bills the insurance company another $100 or $150, depending on the region. The prescription cost is not just the $20 co-pay; it's the $300 cost the pharmacy-benefit manager (PBM) charges the insurance company. Most employees and their dependents don't really know the real cost of their medical care. Nevertheless, when we educate people about their choices and the cost of those choices, then and only then can they be better consumers of their health insurance and know how to better access proper and fair health care.

If you had a choice to pick up one of your generic maintenance prescriptions at a well-known retail pharmacy or get it through a mail-order service but didn't know there was any difference in cost between the two, you would probably go with the "convenient" choice of using the retail pharmacy. However, if you had a financial incentive of zero out-of-pocket and your choice would save money for the plan by going the mail-order route, you might be more inclined to do that. Providing incentive and information is key to helping control the money that goes out of the claims bucket. With the BUCA plans, there is no information, no incentive, and no choice. And it's not about limiting the choices; it is about providing the option to choose. There will be some who don't care and still use the more expensive option, but that's okay: this is America, and the freedom to choose is part of our great country.

If you needed a surgical procedure done, and you would pay your deductible, co-pay, and co-insurance at one provider OR you could go to another provider and didn't have any out of pocket expense, which provider would you go to? Doesn't matter—at least you have the choice. In a BUCA plan, you don't have this choice. You see, in a self-funded plan, the company leadership can design the benefits around their employees or the culture of the company. There is not a BUCA plan that we've seen that covers LASIK eye surgery or bariatric surgery. Conversely, we have clients who include these as routine procedures in their benefit structure. Sure, it's expensive, but because they have self-funded plans, these clients can customize their plans to provide these services. We had a client who wanted to include cochlear implants (expensive hearing aids) in their plan, so they did. Want to provide a minimum-benefit plan but can't afford all the bells and whistles of the BUCA plans? That plan can be designed. Do you have hourly workers who live paycheck to paycheck and can't afford the insurance coverage? There are plan designs that can help with that. Or you can just stay with the BUCAs and their bronze, silver, gold, and platinum plans that are just plain vanilla and too expensive. But you have a choice!

Second, with a self-funded plan, you have more control. What do I mean by that? Have you ever had a great claims year (your broker told you that your loss runs were less than 70 percent) but still had a significant increase on your renewal? How does that make sense? The insurance company made a lot of money on your group that year and still handed you a hefty increase in premium. In this situation, you have no control. Even when your group runs well, you still have to pay more premium. There is no incentive for your employees or their dependents to be concerned about the cost of their medical care. If they use the local big-name pharmacy or get the less expensive mail-order prescription, there is no incentive or consequence for them or for the plan. This type of model breeds apathy. *Who cares? If my choices don't make a difference, if my choices don't have any consequences, why should I make a different decision?*

We have people on benefit plans who are overweight, have high blood pressure, or use tobacco products. What incentive is there for them to change their behavior? There is no incentive and no penalty (except in their personal health) for their actions. Around 20 percent of the people on your plan are spending 82 percent of the claims dollars, and the top 5 percent are spending 50 percent of the claims dollars.[3] That is where the money is. That is where the opportunity is. That is where there needs to be incentives and consequences for choices. In a self-funded plan, you can build in these incentives and consequences. I'm not suggesting that you use a hammer-type penalty to force compliance or coerce people to change their habits. Still, there are ways to help your employees make better decisions and ultimately live healthier lives.

Think about it. If you can change, inspire, or educate part of your workforce to make new decisions on how they access their health care or to change some of their bad habits, you will significantly reduce your claims. And properly implemented incentives as well as penalties for behavior that costs the plan more money can be adopted in self-funded plans. This will have a big impact on your costs.

With a self-funded medical plan, you have more control over plan design, incentives, access to care, and ultimately the costs of your plan. With this model, you have the opportunity to influence people's lives in a positive way.

Finally, you have better communication. This comes in terms of detailed reports and information about utilization, claims, facilities used, and costs of your prescriptions. Communication is the act of imparting or exchanging information. As a CEO, business leader, or HR representative, you regularly look at data. Maybe you look at financial information, production schedules, turnover rates, or other metrics to measure your business. You know what to look at, what to follow, what trends you want to see, and what red flags to keep an eye out for. I bet the one metric you are not watching is in your medical plan. Again, once a year you look at a limited set of information. Your broker brings you the renewal with a long face or set of reasons why your rates have gone up. It's a report, but it has no data or useful information to help you make a new decision. It provides no details or options about what you can do differently to cut costs. With a self-funded medical plan, a sharp broker, and a good third-party administrator (TPA), you will have important information and data on a monthly basis to see the trends, watch what is happening to the dollars in your claims bucket, and evaluate what is driving your costs.

Communication in this area is critical. What other expense do you have as a company that increases as significantly as your medical spending does? Armed with new information, you can make new decisions. Yes, a self-funded plan will require a little more work, as you need to familiarize yourself and your team about what metrics to watch, but it will be well worth your time.

Chapter 4

Two Buckets

Principle 1

In order to fully appreciate the control and choices you have, you need to understand the fundamentals of the self-funded medical-plan model. This chapter will address the first of five principles and will also give insight about the current medical system and its limitations. This principle is the core to a successful future for your medical plan through expanding your choices and helping your employees take ownership of their medical care.

The term *self-funded* contains the first principle you need to grasp. Fund, funded, funding—however you read it, it is about the money. In the fully insured BUCA model, you pay a fixed monthly premium and then that money is dispersed according to the insurance carrier. The carrier pays administration fees, network fees, claims, commissions, prescription costs, and a myriad of other fees and charges. This is the "set it and forget it" model. Your premium is fixed for one year, and the only changes occur because of your employee population. You hire people, and your premiums go up; you fire people, and your premiums go down.

In a self-funded model, the plan can be set up to act in the same way. You pay a fixed amount each month, and the money is used to pay administration fees and claims. The only variance is your employee population. What's the difference in the money? This, my friend, is the point of this whole book! There is a huge difference in the money.

To grasp this principle, we have to know where the money goes. Whether you have a BUCA plan or a self-funded one, the money figuratively goes into two buckets: the administration bucket and the claims bucket. There are only two expense accounts for your premium dollars. Every health-insurance carrier has only two buckets of money, and how much money goes into each bucket and how much money comes out of each bucket is literally the secret that the BUCAs don't want you to know. Certainly, with the Affordable Care Act, there was an attempt to uncover this with the regulations on medical-loss ratios, but that is not the answer. Do you have any more information about your plan costs than you did prior to the ACA? The answer is no. Government regulation hasn't helped you understand any more about the costs of your business's medical plan.

Identifying the two buckets is part of the answer. The first bucket of money is the administration (admin) bucket. This bucket pays for the plan setup: ID cards, EOBs, network-access fees, insurance staff, commissions, customer-service staff, and so on. The second bucket is the claims bucket. This pays for the medical claims from hospitals, doctors, surgery centers, and other places of service. It also pays for the prescriptions your employees need. Your premium dollars are divided into these two buckets. In general, about one-third of the cost is in the admin bucket, and two-thirds are in the claims bucket. And while every dollar in every bucket is important, the first line of attack must be on the claims bucket. This bucket is bigger, and you and your employees have a direct effect on this bucket.

Only Two Buckets of Money

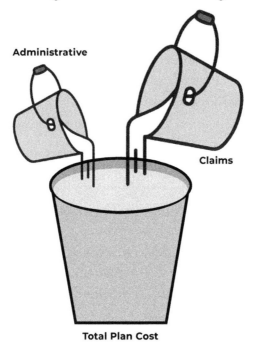

Some brokers and consultants want to spreadsheet these costs and focus your attention on the admin costs. Again, every dollar is important; however, the claims bucket is where you can have the fastest and biggest impact. But many brokers rarely help you with ideas, programs, or ways to reduce the flow of money out of the claims bucket. Our most successful clients recognize that the admin costs must be fair but that the education for decreasing claims costs is the highest priority. We'll address this more in a later chapter.

Your premium dollars conceptually go into these two buckets, and what you need to know is where your money goes literally. When you write a check to a BUCA carrier, *your* money is deposited into *their* bank account. You will never see that money again. It's gone. It's just like Social Security. There is no account at Social Security with *your* money in it.

Where does your money literally go in a self-funded plan? In a self-funded medical plan, *your* money stays in *your* bank account. Let's talk about the process of paying for a self-funded medical plan. First you have a guaranteed maximum cost. Your monthly premiums are calculated based on this maximum plan cost.

You, as the business and plan sponsor, collect the premium dollars. You are sent a monthly invoice for the admin fees (or fixed costs). Remember, this is about one-third of the money you collected. You still have two-thirds of the premium left in *your* bank account. In your medical plan, there is a new partner, the third-party administrator, who acts like the insurance carrier by processing the claims and handling customer service for you. They send you a report on claims that are submitted each week. You then fund the claims payments from the two-thirds of the premium dollars that are in *your* bank account. There is protection built into the plan that helps with cash flow and high claims. Protection will be discussed more in a later chapter.

Here's the point: if you and your employees don't spend the money that is in *your* bank account, that money is *still* in *your* bank account. In a BUCA plan, if there is money left over in the claims bucket, how much of that do they send back to you? That's right—none! They say "Thank you very much," sweep the money out of the account, and still increase your premiums the next year. In a self-funded medical plan, you have a choice, and every decision you and your employees make regarding their health care is a decision that directly affects the claims bucket. This concept is not a magic pill or silver bullet. It's not a plan or course of action for every company. It takes a certain type of company, organization, leadership, culture, and employee to utilize and get the most out of a self-funded medical plan. But all of these concepts can be taught. We have clients in every business segment, and everyone, when given this information, is better equipped to:

1. Understand the health-care market and how to better navigate it
2. Make new decisions regarding their health care
3. Take ownership of their health care

Knowing how the money works, how the money flows, and where the money goes will help you and your employees make better buying decisions related to your medical coverage.

Personal Responsibility

Principle 2

K nowing how the money works and where the money goes in a medical plan is part of the answer. Personal responsibility is the second part of the answer. And this is the second principle of a self-funded medical plan: each individual needs to take ownership of his or her health care. When people know they have choices and that those choices directly affect their wallets, their bank accounts, and the cash in their pockets, they make different decisions. In the current medical system, no one sees how their decisions influence anything. When a person has a medical need, he or she goes to the doctor, presents a medical ID card, and "gets" something: a doctor's (or in many cases a physician assistant's) advice or diagnosis, a prescription, or a recommendation to go see a specialist. Beyond that, most people are very uneducated about the medical system, costs, and health care in general. We spend more time analyzing, evaluating, and mulling over a vehicle purchase than we give to our health-care decisions. Why? Because we have been taught that by showing a little card, everything is taken care of—for now. Health care is so much more than that. In some plans today, a family will spend more than $30,000 (premiums, co-pays, co-insurance, and so on) *before* the insurance plan kicks in a dollar. And, unfortunately, when we need the information, it's too late. Because we're in a medical crisis and we have to go to the doctor or hospital, there's no time to research or consider the consequences of our decisions. After we receive the care is when we get information on how our health insurance will pay for those decisions. For many families, this is when the trouble begins. As if the medical issue was not concern enough, now they have to worry about paying for it. "In 2017, 31% of the insured found it difficult to afford copays.... Similarly, 43% found deductibles too high."[1] The Kaiser Family Foundation also found that in 2015, medical bills were a major cause for bankruptcy, even beyond credit card debt or mortgage default.[2]

Human nature seems to force us to take the path of least resistance, the most convenient path. We've been taught that those little ID cards we carry in our wallets are how we get our medical care, or at least it gives us access to medical care. And those little cards dictate *who* gives us care. But it provides no options or alternatives for our care. It gives us no information about the consequences of our choices. We only know that we give the doctor the little card and we get care. Yes, it is convenient, and we don't have to think about our decisions, but there is a price for convenience. The power of choice is what drives our free-market economy. You can travel by car, bus, train, commercial airplane, or private airplane to get to a destination. Each of these options has a convenience factor and a price. Let me illustrate this. Recently I flew from Los Angeles to Dallas and then on to Tulsa. I paid a reasonable fare and it took me about six hours to get to my destination. I could have taken a bus and it would have cost me about half as much money, but it would have taken five times as long. Conversely, I could have chartered a private jet, which certainly would have been more convenient and less stressful, and the journey would have taken about three hours, but it would have cost me about ten times as much as my commercial flight. Each option in my travel had its convenience factor and cost factor.

Our health-care decisions have the same two factors: convenience and cost. We can't go online and "shop" for our medical care. If the government stays out of the mix, the day will come that market pressure will force providers to compete on quality, cost, and convenience. And choosing the self-funded medical-plan model can accelerate the process of giving your employees choices while helping them realize the consequences. Your employees can make their choices based on cost and convenience, and you can protect the plan, your plan, by adding controls and incentives so that each person will pay the appropriate amount. In the travel example, should I demand that I get the convenience of a three-hour flight on a private jet at the same cost of the bus ride? No! No one in his or her right mind would expect that. However, many politicians are telling everyone that we should have the great medical system we have today and that no one should have to pay more. There is a *cost* to quality and convenience.

This ignorance is the reason we don't understand why premiums keep going up faster than inflation, why the government can't fix the problem, and why you as a business owner or leader have not had better choices. Let's remove the ignorance and give people the education they need to make new decisions and fix this broken system.

Gaining a broader understanding of the fundamentals of a

self-funded medical plan will enable you to make new choices in how you provide the medical care for your employees. Helping employees understand and take responsibility for both their medical care and the financial consequences of their choices will make them wiser consumers of their health care, and a smarter consumer will help improve the economic system. Then everyone wins.

Cost shifting, the methodology to controlling costs given by the BUCAs over the past ten years, is not what this is referring to. If cost shifting really worked, we would see better premiums and lower costs. But we all know that has not happened. One way to reduce costs is to limit utilization, basically telling people not to go to the doctor. And this is what cost shifting is really telling people. That will certainly reduce overall costs, but it will not improve people's health.

For decades, life-insurance companies have charged more for people who smoke. The nonsmokers get lower premiums than smokers. Why? Because medical science has documented that smoking reduces one's life expectancy. So actuarially, the life-insurance companies need more premium from smokers to cover the costs of smoking.

Now, this next statement is neither politically correct nor nondiscriminatory: individuals need to take responsibility for their health, and they should pay premiums and share the costs of their decisions. If 20 percent of the people would change their lifestyle, that would positively affect about 80 percent of the health-care spending in our country. There are about five chronic conditions that account for 75 percent of health-care spending: heart disease, cancer, diabetes, arthritis, and obesity.[3]

"Chronic diseases are the most common and costly of all

health problems, but they are also the most preventable.... Our common, health-damaging, but modifiable behaviors— tobacco use, insufficient physical activity, poor eating habits, and excessive alcohol use—are responsible for much of the illness, disability, and premature death related to chronic disease.... Ten percent of the population consumes 63% of the total health care dollars in the country."[4]

Yes, individual decisions have consequences. If you choose to eat at a five-star restaurant, you are choosing to pay the bill at the end of the dinner. If you choose to smoke, you are making a health-care decision. If you choose to overeat on a regular basis, you are making a health-care decision. Certainly, there are medical issues that are not someone's choice. A five-year-old having leukemia is not a lifestyle choice by the five-year-old. An athlete who is a sophomore in high school having diabetes is not a lifestyle choice.

Consider these statistics:

- 34.3 million people (age 18 and older) used cigarettes in 2017.[5]
- More than 16 million Americans live with smoking-related diseases.[6]
- 3.4% of adults used smokeless tobacco in 2016.[7]
- In 2018 over 39% of adults and 18% of children were considered obese.[8]
- In 2015 over 30 million adults had diabetes.[9]
- In 2015 over 84 million people in the US were identified as having prediabetes.[10]
- In 2015, 26.9 percent of people age 18 or older reported that they engaged in binge drinking in the

past month; 7 percent reported that they engaged in heavy alcohol use in the past month.[11]

However, you want to count the total, there are many people who engage in these four health-damaging behaviors. And how much do these behaviors cost our medical system and work productivity?

- Smoking costs more than $326 Billion
  - ► $170 Billion in direct medical costs
  - ► $156 Billion in lost productivity costs[12]
- $263 Billion on Obesity expenditures or 7.9% of the total medical spending in 2015[13]
  - ► $190 Billion in direct medical costs[14]
  - ► $73 Billion in lost productivity costs[15]
- Diabetes costs more than $327 Billion
  - ► $237 Billion in direct medical costs
  - ► $90 Billion in lost productivity costs[16]
- Alcoholism costs more than $249 Billion
  - ► $149 Billion in medical, legal, and related costs
  - ► $100 Billion in lost productivity costs[17]

The economic impact of these four behaviors is huge. Going back to an earlier chapter, the total medical spending in the US was $3.5 trillion in 2017. These four health issues account for a staggering $735 billion or 21 percent of the direct medical spending. And they account for another $419 billion dollars in workplace lost productivity.

Yes, personal responsibility does play a huge part in our overall health and the costs.

Protection

Principle 3

The third principle of a self-funded medical plan is the concept of protection. Though the model contains the word *self*, it doesn't necessarily mean self-insured. When the idea of self-funding a medical plan first came around, the plans were truly self-insured. Only big companies such as AT&T, U.S. Steel, General Motors, Chase Bank, and Chevron Corporation could financially participate in that model. They would pay the claims from their cash flow, as they had the financial capacity to absorb an expensive claim. Today there are numerous insurance carriers that provide coverage appropriate for all sizes of self-funded medical plans. Because more insurance companies participate in this market, they have designed policies that work for smaller companies. There is even a carrier that will self-fund a group of two employees. A more accurate term for today's self-funded medical plans designed for companies other than the Fortune 500 is, partially self-funded.

Let's dig into the mechanics of a self-funded medical plan and how the plan itself is protected. It is this concept of protection that most brokers, HR directors, and company leaders don't understand. The self-funded medical plans offered today have two primary levels of insurance: one level addresses the individual participant, and another level protects the overall plan. This coverage is called stop-loss insurance and helps minimize risk. As a business owner or leader, you can accept or transfer as much or as little risk as you want. This is another way you can control costs and customize the plan to fit your company.

There are other terms that denote the same type of insurance coverage. A couple of these are excess insurance and reinsurance. Although this may be a new concept for many readers, this type of insurance has actually been around for hundreds of years. As long ago as 1799, Germany, Switzerland, and England were some of the first places where reinsurance carriers started. Today some of the largest reinsurance carriers are Swiss RE, Munich RE, Berkshire Hathaway, China RE, Lloyd's of London, Reinsurance Group of America, Chubb Limited, and Sirius International.[1]

Reinsurance is a fancy term for transferring risk. Many of us have heard about catastrophic losses created by Hurricanes Katrina, Harvey, Sandy, and Maria. How did the insurance companies—such as State Farm, Allstate, and Farmers—survive such disasters? The answer: reinsurance. Reinsurance is insurance for insurance companies. Life insurance carriers have used this for years to protect their block of business. A company may retain the first million dollars of exposure, but then a reinsurance carrier picks up any additional risk or loss over the first million dollars. In hurricane-prone areas, a company such as State Farm may have taken the first $500 million of loss and then their reinsurance carrier picked up the rest. Consider this concept like a deductible, such as the one you have on your auto insurance. The reinsurance is set up so the insured has a large deductible.

In the same way, a self-funded medical program will keep the first portion of the risk and then transfer the rest of the risk (the potential loss over the deductible amount) to another insurance carrier. There is premium cost involved in this, and it is part of your fixed-costs bucket. That is the nature of insurance: we pay a small premium for a safety net, and the insurance company assumes the risk of the larger claims cost.

For the self-funded medical plan, there is an insurance policy that will cover each individual. This is called specific stop-loss, and a deductible is chosen for each individual. For small companies, this is around $25,000. For bigger companies, this figure may be more like $100,000, $250,000, or more per medical-plan member. This amount of money is what the plan must pay before the insurance will kick in and contribute. When a member exceeds the deductible amount in medical expenses, the reinsurance carrier pays everything over that amount for covered benefits. Now, before you stop reading and say that is ridiculous, keep going, because the figures will start to make sense a little later.

The second type of insurance protection around the self-funded plan is aggregate stop-loss. An aggregate is the cumulative total. This represents the maximum the plan will pay into the claims bucket. If the claims for the entire group or company exceed this maximum, the aggregate stop-loss pays the claims over the maximum. Just like your current BUCA plan, a self-funded medical plan has a maximum expense. Thus, you can plan and budget around this number. Regardless of what happens in terms of each specific loss, the plan is protected and will not pay beyond the aggregate total.

Let's discuss a couple of examples. Let's assume you are a small company and have a specific deductible of $25,000. One of your employees has a medical condition that requires surgery. The claims between the hospital, doctor, anesthesiologist, and imaging total $36,000. The plan would pay the first $25,000 from the claims bucket. The additional $11,000 would be paid by the reinsurance carrier as a specific, or spec, claim. If that same employee then had another issue after this first surgery that required prescription drugs amounting to $1,100 per month, this cost would also be covered by the reinsurance contract. This concept is applied to each member, not just each employee, who is on your medical plan.

Let's make another assumption. You have a total of one hundred members (fifty employees and fifty dependents on your plan, just to make it easy). Quick math will tell you that if all one hundred members reached the specific deductible, the plan would be responsible for $2,500,000 of claims cost. And your experience tells you that you don't spend that much on your BUCA-plan premiums. How do we reconcile the cost differential?

This is where the aggregate stop-loss comes into play. The reinsurance carrier has calculated a maximum claims figure. This is called the maximum exposure. This is also called the attachment point. Once your plan reaches this amount, it is fully funded and you will not pay any more claims costs from your claims bucket. Again, based on a company with one hundred plan members, let's say that your maximum claims cost was $400,000 and your total administration cost was

$285,000. Your maximum cost with both the admin bucket and the claims bucket is therefore $685,000. In this scenario, your attachment point would be $400,000.

Theoretically, you could put $685,000 into a bank account and never put in another dollar. If you had sixteen members reach their specific deductible of $25,000, that would be $400,000 out of the claims bucket. Guess what? That is all your plan would have to pay for the group. All the other claims would be paid by the stop-loss carrier. While it is highly unlikely there would be that many spec claims in a group of this size, this shows how the plan works with the specific deductible and the aggregate deductible.

Think about each of these as a "super" deductible. One is for each individual (spec, or specific), and the other is a deductible for the entire group (the agg, or aggregate). Once the plan pays the deductibles, the reinsurance carrier takes over.

What does this mean in practical terms? Your self-funded medical plan is protected just like the BUCA plans. Blue Cross, UnitedHealthcare, Cigna, and Aetna all have reinsurance for their block of medical plans. How they design their reinsurance program may be different just due to size, but the general principle is the same: they transfer the risk at some level.

As you consider a self-funded medical plan, remember there is insurance that sits as a backstop behind your plan. This insurance protects the plan and puts a limit on your exposure to the risk of unknown medical claims. The principle of protection will allow you to make this important decision about whether or not to install a self-funded medical plan based on other factors. While a BUCA plan is a "set it and forget it" type of plan, there is no opportunity for savings or any way to cut claims and thus the renewal and future costs. The self-funded plan is protected like a BUCA plan with reinsurance that limits your exposure and the risk you take. Thus, if you spend all the money in the claims bucket, the insurance will kick in and fund the rest of the claims. But if you don't spend all the money in your claims bucket you get to keep all the money

The principle of protection is very important. There are brokers out there who will use the security of a BUCA plan to scare you into believing that a self-funded plan is risky. Yet through plan design, reinsurance and other insurance like Transplant policies, a self-funded plan can be just as secure and safe and with a financial upside. When you know about the options, have freedom to design your own program, educate and encourage employees how to get involved, you can leverage your employee benefit program as a huge positive for your employees while reducing and/or controlling the expense.

Chapter 7

Choices

Principle 4

The fourth principle that is foundational to a self-funded medical plan is that of choice. The BUCA plans focus on networks and little ID cards in our pockets that give us access to a certain number of doctors and facilities. We have unknowingly been taught that this network is everything we need. If we stay within the confines of the network, we can have anything done, our every medical need taken care of, and nothing to worry about. Show our ID cards, and the magical land of medicine is opened and made available to us.

Because of cost shifting and the ever-increasing cost of medical care, the BUCAs have moved to a philosophy of a narrow network. They offer lower-priced plans to the employer groups (your company) if you accept the limited number of providers. Instead of all four hospitals in your area, maybe only one or two are in network. Instead of twelve cardiologists, maybe only three are in this network.

The BUCAs try to control costs by limiting the number of options in the network. They do this by offering only super-preferred providers because these providers give the BUCAs the highest discounts. Remember our discussion about discounts in an earlier chapter? Discounts are just a shell game used to convince decision makers that the BUCA's network is the most cost effective.

We need to have the flag of choice in one hand and the flag of personal responsibility in the other hand. Hardworking men and women all around the country are being duped by the BUCAs because of the little cards in their pockets that they've come to believe are their tickets to health care. On one hand, they're told to take care of their health and get the medical care they need; on the other hand, they're handed these little cards that are the gatekeepers that limit their choices.

But it's not completely the fault of the BUCAs, as the providers have their share of culpability. For instance, there are fourteen automobile manufacturers in the United States that produce thirty-five brands that account for 99 percent of the cars sold in America.[1] We can purchase a brand-new car for as little as fourteen thousand dollars or as much as a couple millions of dollars. We know this because there is a price tag and we can see the price. Where else in the world do we make a purchasing decision and then weeks later get a bill to see how much it cost? Nowhere, except in the medical/health field. Again, the providers have been willing participants in this shell game in that we don't know the price of anything.

However, we can't stop there. There is a third party who is also a participant and thereby responsible in this scenario. Yes, it's you and me. We are the consumers, and up until now, we have gone along with this system because the system worked, to a point, and we (the companies we work for and our families) could handle the costs. We have reached a point where the costs and the continued rising costs are becoming unbearable.

Sounds like a perfect scenario for the government to step in and fix it, right? Not! Having the government step in with a one-payer system is just furthering the ignorance. How many people on Medicare or Medicaid care about the costs? Who is motivated in that system to take care of their health and make good decisions? Is anyone incentivized to do the right thing? Of course, the answer to all these questions is a resounding no!

Education, personal responsibility, and information makes up the formula for success in this health-care system. There is one more item that I need to address. The medical system is complex in terms of diagnosis, CPT and DRG codes, and all the related services that go along with this. Our ignorance is partly due to the nature of the situation. Unless we were human-anatomy or biology majors in college, we know relatively little about how our physical bodies work, function, or deal with sickness. That is partly why doctors, who have invested significant time and money for their educations, are respected as "experts." As a result, most of us have relegated our health knowledge to the experts and thereby abdicated to others our responsibility for our health care. That's why we need to be more educated consumers.

We must start somewhere and become better consumers of our health-care system. Reading this book is a great start because you are being exposed to inside information and given a perspective on how the system works. In order to become a better consumer, you must know about the choices you have and what they cost.

For the consumer, resources such as Amazon and eBay have created a new way to compare and see what the fair market price is for specific goods. You can search for an item on Amazon and find a dozen sellers, and the prices offered may vary by 5 to 50 percent for the same item. If you're looking to purchase a vintage automobile or truck in your area, you can look on eBay and see what a similar vehicle is selling for in other areas. Then you have the information to determine if you're getting a good deal or if you will have to pay a premium to get the truck you want.

Unfortunately, there is no eBay or Amazon for our medical care. There is no way to compare prices. The only price most of us know is our co-pay. That's what we pay, but that is not the price. There is a second bill that is sent to the insurance company, and this constitutes the rest of the price. This is revealed to you and me when we get that pesky form in the mail called an Explanation of Benefits. And most of us don't understand this form because of all the codes on the page. Usually we only care about one thing: whether or not we owe the doctor more money.

But isn't it a crazy system where we make a purchasing decision, get the service, and then get the bill weeks later? What would our food-distribution and grocery system look like if we went to the store, loaded our baskets with food that wasn't priced, paid a fixed co-pay at the register, and got the rest of the bill in the mail a week later? The grocery man would be chasing the customers to get the rest of his money, consumers wouldn't go to the store when they needed to because they were scared of the bill that might come later, and the grocery store would have to charge more money to be profitable because of so many people not being able or willing to pay for their groceries.

And although you say that would be a preposterous system,

that is exactly what happens with our medical system. Wouldn't it be awesome if we could get a medical procedure done and know the cost up front? Wouldn't it be great if we could go to the doctor with confidence and know we wouldn't get this huge bill in the mail weeks later that we were responsible to pay? Wouldn't it be amazing if we could order our prescription and know that we were paying a fair price?

Visit the Surgery Center of Oklahoma's website and see the prices listed for their surgeries. When you use a pharmacy-benefit manager such as MaxCare, Drexi, or Southern Scripts, you can see for yourself that they make money only on the admin fee they charge the plan. Use other PBMs and they will make money on your plan in thirty different ways beyond the admin fee.

The good news is that you have a choice. All this is possible with a self-funded medical plan. But you must be willing to get out of the BUCA model, escape the confines of how we've been conditioned to use the little plastic cards in our pockets, and take personal responsibility. Then and only then will you truly have choices regarding your medical care.

Chapter 8

Controls

Principle 5

The fifth and final principle of a self-funded medical program is controls. In any good process or system, there have to be checkpoints, measurements, and ways to monitor progress, whether success or failure. As insurance has developed over the last hundred years, deductibles have been used to curb abuse and "provide a cushion between any given minimal loss and a true catastrophic loss."[1] The foundation of insurance is that it should provide help when there is a catastrophe. Insurance was never meant to be a checkbook for every little loss or unforeseen cost. So many politicians, media outlets, and other voices are unwittingly promoting a system that is not insurance at all. They are promoting a system that denies personal responsibility and promotes ignorance.

Forty years ago, the very name of our insurance coverage was an indication of this. It was called our *major*-medical insurance. It was not designed to cover every doctor's appointment, every little procedure, and every prescription. PPO models, provider chargemasters and our desire for security, safety, and ease has driven us to the "fiscal cliff," where these covered costs have created an insatiable monster. We call this monster our modern health-insurance system.

The BUCAs offer us such controls as deductibles, co-pays, and out-of-pocket expenses. That's because their system will allow for only these types of controls. Let's consider the business practices of Southwest Airlines. Why is the company so successful, and why can't the other airlines compete? The answer is simple: Southwest built a new system and didn't copy the business model of the other airlines. Southwest used only one type of airplane. Southwest focused on shorter routes to give people who would normally drive the option to fly. Southwest developed a system of keeping their airplanes in the air and not sitting too long at the terminal. Because the company started with just three airplanes, money would be made only when those planes were in the air. Today Southwest Airlines has a turnaround process at the gate and terminal that no other airline can compete with. Why? Because they have processes and controls in place that the other airlines can't use because of the confines of their "systems."

In a similar way, the BUCAs have a system in place that has limits. Their system is not designed to educate. It is not designed to help anyone save money. It is not designed to promote choices and personal responsibility or good health. Let's be honest—the current BUCA system makes money only when people are sick. So, in a demented way, the BUCAs really want more sick and injured people.

What if we could access health care with a different system and different processes? What if employers and employees had other incentives and more information? This what-if is not just a dream or theory; it can be a reality for you. And as with

Southwest Airlines, it will take a little courage and toughness to break out of the system, to bend the system, and to compete and win financially. This means finding ways within the health-care world to redefine how we access services and what amount of money we pay for those services. Southwest Airlines still must comply with the Federal Aviation Administration. Likewise, a self-funded medical plan has to comply with various regulations and laws. But there is a different system available.

How can employees and their dependents be motivated to learn about and take advantage of new options? Companies can incentivize employees to utilize certain providers by changing, reducing, or removing co-pays. This provides two choices: use certain providers with no co-pay or deductible or use other providers and pay co-pays and deductibles. That's a strong incentive and a new control.

Providing employees and dependents with new methods of interacting with doctors for routine services is another control. This may come in the form of a company doctor, a telemedicine doctor, or a direct primary-care physician. With the first of these three options, larger companies have a dedicated doctor, either on-site or in a local office, whose practice is focused on that company or a fixed group of companies. The benefits of this arrangement are convenience, engagement, lower costs, better outcomes, more attentive care, and less stress for the patient. Some examples of these types of providers are CareATC, MedCor, OnSite Care, and Premise Health. Smaller companies can participate in this model as well. They may share medical providers or contract with other companies to finance doctors or clinics dedicated to their group of companies. This model will give you monthly data on utilization and associated costs.

Another way employees interact with doctors is through telemedicine, which is the use of telecommunications technology to diagnose and treat patients remotely. This has been around for a few years, and almost every state now allows this type of medical care for routine medical issues. Telemedicine can be used to diagnose about 70 percent of what a primary-care physician would diagnose in person at his or her office. For young adults and many other groups, the convenience and effectiveness of this style of care is beyond measure. According to one report, there are more than 275 telemedicine providers now.[2] This list is growing, as the BUCAs are recognizing the value of this type of care and offering it in their medical plans. Some of the best telemedicine providers are Teladoc, HealthiestYou, PlushCare, Doctor on Demand, and MDLIVE. And the best part of this for you, the employer, is information and savings. You can access reports on telemedicine utilization. Each time an employee or dependent uses the service, it saves you and your medical plan money. This is meaningful if you have a self-funded medical plan. If you reduce costs, you save money. It's a direct relationship. But in a BUCA plan, this doesn't happen, because of their system and its limitations. With a BUCA plan, you never take part in the savings of such programs.

A third way for employees to receive medical treatment is through direct primary care, in which patients have access to care through a monthly membership fee, access fee, or retainer. Doctors who practice direct primary care find it a great alternative to the fee-for-services model that the BUCAs offer. Members pay a monthly fee to the doctor who becomes their concierge primary-care physician. Although there are limitations to this service, it is really the old-fashioned family-doctor model. It provides better access, less waiting time, and more personalized service. Companies that utilize this type of service find that their employees have better care and are more willing to go to the doctor when they really need to. This can potentially save the plan, as small medical issues won't develop into big medical issues because of lack of care.

Each of these three types of services offers a new way for accessing medical care. The BUCA system drives patients down an assembly line. How many times have you gone to the doctor's office to talk to your physician about a medical concern, only to be seen by their PA or for only a few minutes? Unfortunately, service seems to be going down while prices continue to go up. This is a bad model.

A self-funded medical plan can provide options for routine doctor's visits. And with the aforementioned programs, these options make a difference financially in your claims bucket and in the health of your employees. What about the more expensive claims, such as surgeries and chronic illnesses? There are new options, systems, and procedures that can be adopted that will motivate and reward good behavior and save your company money.

Many doctors and surgeons are frustrated with the current health-insurance system, tired of dealing with the BUCAs, and maverick enough to make a change. They want improved patient interaction and they want fair reimbursements. Ask most doctors and the scenario is the same: they have more administrative employees dealing with the insurance claims and payments than they have medical staff dealing with patients. What's wrong with this picture? It's the system—again.

There is a growing number of doctors and surgery centers who:

1. Show their prices up front
2. Are organized for efficiency and great patient outcomes
3. Won't play the BUCA negotiation game
4. Won't Increase their chargemasters after the BUCAs beat them up for more discount

These direct-pay providers take care of the more expensive surgeries and procedures at a fair-market price. Though they don't file the claims with the BUCAs, you as the patient can file the claim and get reimbursed. Let me give you some examples.

BUCA Pricing		Direct-Pay Pricing	
Knee Arthroscopy	$8,226	Knee Arthroscopy	$3,740
Gallbladder Surgery	$13,878	Gallbladder Surgery	$5,865
Hysterectomy	$11,043	Hysterectomy	$8,000
Physical Therapy	$136	Physical Therapy	$80
Anterior Discectomy	$13,355	Anterior Discectomy	$8,855

If your plan was set up properly, if you had controls and incentives in place, and if your plan was rewarded for saving money, wouldn't you *choose* to save money? Now, you might be a little skeptical, because you know the games played in the past inside the health system. But I can assure you, the examples listed above are real, and the facilities are state-of-the-art, modern facilities that will pass any regulatory inspection. We have a significant database of claims to know that the left-side numbers are real. We also have direct-provider contracts in place for our clients to get the pricing on the right side—all day, every day, every member. Employees and their dependents have a choice of where to go. If they choose to go with the left column, they have co-pays, deductibles, and co-insurance. If they have a favorite doctor, they can choose to go to that provider. There's just a different price to pay.

If members instead choose to go to one of the facilities listed on the right column, there are no co-pays, no deductibles, and no co-insurance. You might wonder, *How can the plan afford this?* and that's a great question. Here are three examples of how the plan might work.

Gallbladder	PROCEDURE	Gallbladder
$13,878	CLAIMS COST	$5,865
	(Net minus PPO discount)	
$100	CO-PAY	$0
$2,500	DEDUCTIBLE	$0
$2,276	CO-INSURANCE	$0
	(20 percent in this case)	
$4,8756	PATIENT RESPONSIBILITY	$0
$9,022	PLAN PAYMENT	$5,865
$0	Net Plan Savings	$3,157

BENEFITS Re-Imagined

Hysterectomy	PROCEDURE	Hysterectomy
$11,043	CLAIMS COST	$8,000
	(Net minus PPO discount)	
$100	CO-PAY	$0
$1,500	DEDUCTIBLE	$0
$1,909	CO-INSURANCE	$0
	(20 percent in this case)	
$3,509	PATIENT RESPONSIBILITY	$0
$7,534	PLAN PAYMENT	$8,000
$0	Net Plan Savings	-$466

Anterior Discectomy	PROCEDURE	Anterior Discectomy
$13,355	CLAIMS COST	$8,855
	(Net minus PPO discount)	
$100	CO-PAY	$0
$2,000	DEDUCTIBLE	$0
$2,271	CO-INSURANCE	$0
	(20 percent in this case)	
$4,371	PATIENT RESPONSIBILITY	$0
$8,984	PLAN PAYMENT	$8,855
$0	Net Plan Savings	$129

These three examples were chosen to show the diversity and result of each of the procedures and some of the controls that a plan could have. First, you will notice that not every procedure saved the plan money. Second, we used different plan designs as a point of illustration. Beyond the financial impact of direct contracts, there is a huge psychological impact. Take, for example, the second procedure, the hysterectomy. If an employee or dependent needed this procedure, there are significant health issues. There is recovery time and certainly financial implications. Using the PPO/BUCA side of the equation, this family would be looking down the barrel of a $3,500 expense along with the physical and emotional adjustments. Looking at the direct-pay option, the family has no expense and will deal with just the physical and emotional transition and healing. Is your employee's sanity and well-being worth $466 to you as the CEO, CFO, or HR director?

When we did the analysis on pregnancies and deliveries in this direct-pay model for one of our clients, they broke even on the cost. With the co-pays and co-insurance waived and the direct-contract pricing, the plan broke even. No savings and no additional costs over the BUCA PPO model. However, the goodwill and enhanced benefit to the employees and their spouses was immeasurable. They were able to celebrate their new babies without the additional burden and financial responsibility of the co-pays, co-insurance, and deductibles.

Certainly, there is a balance between giving away benefits and protecting the plan, but only in a self-funded plan do you have this choice. And like any plan, these surgical procedures have the control of pre-certification. An employee or dependent can't just go have a procedure done without it being medically necessary. And to protect the plan, you might choose to have a reduced co-pay rather than no co-pay associated with these direct-pay procedures. Yet that is the beauty of a self-funded model. The creative options are almost endless. If you wanted to pay 100 percent and give the patient $500 for knee surgeries completed on the first Tuesday after a full moon, you could. While this may seem a little absurd, you get the point.

Finally, as we've worked through some of these controls, you've been exposed to the underlying control of information and reports. The biggest control you have is information, and lack of information is one of the biggest limitations in a BUCA plan. Engaging in a self-funded medical plan will require someone to take ownership of the information and make decisions from it. When you see trends, that is new information for making new decisions. You might do nothing, and that's fine. Or you may want to adjust the plan. But at least you have the information to make a decision and the freedom to make a change.

Chapter 9

Final Thoughts

Throughout this book, you've been introduced to new information and given ideas to ponder. This resource is meant to be an introduction to self-funded medical plans. It's difficult to cover all the options of a self-funded medical plan, as each situation requires a different set of priorities to make it fit your company and employees. In this final chapter, there are a few more concepts to present. Whether you continue to work with your current broker or seek out another resource, these additional ideas will help you ask necessary questions and be better prepared to make new decisions.

In the discussion of alternative medical plans, there are some very important ideas to explore. These will be addressed over the next few pages.

PRESCRIPTION DRUGS

About 20 to 30 percent of your medical plan spending can be for the prescription drugs your employees and their dependents use. There are three primary players in the delivery system for our drugs: the manufacturer, the pharmacy-benefit manager, and the pharmacy. Most individuals know where to get their prescriptions, but that is the extent of their knowledge and experience. Other than through advertisements on TV, most people don't even know about the drug manufacturers. Without going into mind-numbing detail, here's a brief tutorial on the prescription-drug world.

Manufacturer

The company that does research and development of new drugs is called the manufacturer. Their product is a specific drug that solves or helps with a medical issue. Pfizer, Novartis, Roche Holding, Merck, Johnson & Johnson, GlaxoSmithKline, and Eli Lilly are some of the largest pharmaceutical companies in the world.[1] These companies spend millions of dollars researching new drugs for various applications. Eliquis, Entresto, Humira, and Keytruda are just a few of these drugs. Because of regulations, consumers can't purchase their drugs directly from the manufacturer.

Pharmacy-Benefit Manager

The PBM is the middleman in the equation and can be considered a distributor that has accumulated buying power. They distribute the prescription drugs to the pharmacies. Because of their position, they receive the manufacturer rebates. How much they keep or pass along to you is up to them. This is an area of profiteering and limited transparency. However, there are some transparent PBMs, and their value is unmatched. This is an important topic to discuss with your broker.

Pharmacy

The pharmacy is the final element in the delivery system, as it is the pickup location for your prescription. Pharmacies pay for the drug, which covers the ingredient cost. The pharmacy also gets a fee for their services, normally called a dispensing fee.

While these are the players in the drug-delivery system, it is so much more complex than this. Because of such terms as *federal upper limit, maximum allowable cost, average wholesale price*, and *average actual cost*, figuring out the inner workings of the PBM and overall prescription-drug world can be a daunting task. There are four elements that you need to know and discuss with your broker to manage and maximize this part of your medical plan and spending:

1. Ingredient costs: manufacturer
2. Pickup options: pharmacy/mail order
3. Drug therapies
4. Rebates: manufacturer and PBM

There are also some new drugs on the market or coming to market that you need to be aware of for your plan. These drugs, while very effective, are so expensive that they can crater any plan. One of the key roles of your third-party administrator is to provide a list of these drugs and make recommendations for plan amendments that may exclude these drugs to help avoid the financial ramifications. When a plan excludes these drugs, often the manufacturer will provide assistance through the PBM so the member can get them.

COSTS

The costs associated with most self-funded medical plans are comparable with the fully insured BUCA plans that you have purchased in the past. The perception is that a self-funded medical plan is more expensive. However, the truth is that you have more information to control the costs, your employees have choices that directly affect the claims bucket, and there is insurance that protects the plan from claims over the deductibles. How you track and analyze your medical costs is vital to your success. You need to evaluate the programs and options on a regular basis to see the impact on the claims bucket.

RISK

By using a self-funded plan, you are assuming a different kind of risk than with a traditional BUCA plan. There is an aura of security and safety with a fully insured BUCA plan. Costs are fixed and guaranteed. Nothing is going to happen that will blow up the plan or put your organization at risk. Your employees have their marching orders: "Stay in network and your out-of-pocket expenses are fixed." That philosophy is fine until you can't afford the coverage—until your employees don't enroll in the benefits due to cost or you have to cut staff to cover the rising costs of health care. Unfortunately, that's where so many companies are today. Too many organizations are making tough decisions just to keep their medical plan.

Certainly, there are risks in a self-funded plan. But there is insurance that helps protect your self-funded plan, and there is a plan document that sets the limits and provides a legal basis for your plan and what claims are eligible. The risks involved in a plan of this type are:

1. Noncompliance: Employees are free to choose, and their choices may cost the plan more money in terms of claims.
2. Lifestyle: There are unhealthy lifestyles that affect a member's health. The claims bucket will be negatively affected by the number of members you have in this category.
3. Shock claim: This is an unusually high claim. An ongoing expensive medical issue will have a huge impact on the claims bucket and the renewal. A couple of years ago, one of our clients had one such claim. The dependent of a C-suite executive needed a drug therapy that cost more than a million dollars. The plan and related premiums couldn't absorb this additional million-dollar hit, so the client had no choice but to go back to a BUCA carrier.

APPRECIATION FOR THE BUCAS

Throughout this book, much has been said about the BUCA carriers. Blue Cross (Anthem, Blue Shield), UnitedHealthcare, Cigna, and Aetna have played a major role in our current health-insurance system. As health care changed, they changed. As regulations required different results, they changed. When Baylor University sold its first program in 1929, it was revolutionary and helped thousands of people access good health care. Today some people wouldn't have medical insurance if it weren't for the BUCA plans. The philosophy outlined in these pages does not advocate getting rid of the BUCA carriers. They are essential to our medical insurance system and health-care delivery. However, there needs to be changes in the areas of transparency, costs, incentives, controls, and information.

SELF-FUNDED MEDICAL PLAN: A NEW WAY

Medical technology is advancing so fast that government approval and acceptance can't keep up. That is why this book is more about a philosophy than about a specific process. If you keep in mind that it is your health, your money, and your choice, you will make different decisions. If the government gives us universal health insurance, then it becomes no one's health care. It is no one's responsibility. It's the government's responsibility and cost. That is the most dangerous place for our health care and our health-insurance system.

What has been outlined in this book is a way of thinking and a way of life. As Americans, we have the most freedom of any nation in the world, but with that freedom comes great responsibility. Our health-care-delivery system definitely needs help. Our health-insurance system needs an overhaul! There are too many greedy, profit-motivated, big-money decision makers controlling the system. When each of us stands up, uses this information, and makes new decisions, we will see a change. To be sure, this change will not happen overnight. However, one person at a time, one claim at a time, one company at a time that uses these principles will have an effect, and this will create a ripple and then a wave and then a tsunami of change.

You've been equipped with new information, new options, and new ideas. Make a new decision today. Start by asking questions. Start by asking your broker or consultant about these ideas. Have the courage to fire your broker or consultant if he or she won't give you the answers, can't give you the answers, or is unwilling to show you options beyond the BUCAs.

All of us have a vested interest in our health care and health insurance. Insurance plays an important role in how people take care of their health and medical issues. Knowing how the system works, what motivates certain decisions, and where the money goes is important for unlocking your choices and making the system better. Health-insurance carriers, agents, brokers, providers, and consumers all have responsibility to each other. In the end, it's not about assigning blame or casting stones at the guilty; it is about finding a new way, having complete information, and working with each other for the good of everyone involved.

ADDITIONAL READING

"High Cost Claims and Injectable Drug Trends," Sun Life Financial, https://orders.wilde.com/viewvalidpdf_UWilde .asp?productid=146779&GoBackTo=noEditPart.asp.

Agency for Healthcare Research and Quality, U.S. Department of Health and Human Services, https://www .ahrq.gov/.

Tim Sandle, "Op-Ed: Knowledge Doubles Almost Every Day, and It's Set to Increase," *Digital Journal*, November 23, 2018, http://www.digitaljournal.com/tech-and-science/science/op-ed -knowledge-doubles-almost-every-day-and-it-s-set-to-increase /article/537543.

"Infographic—US Health Care Spending: Who Pays?," California Health Care Foundation, May 22, 2019, https:// www.chcf.org/publication/us-health-care-spending-who-pays/.

"Health Effects of Cigarette Smoking," Centers for Disease Control and Prevention, https://www.cdc.gov/tobacco

/data_statistics/fact_sheets/health_effects/effects_cig_smoking
/index.htm.

Peter Loftus, "Drugmakers Are Lobbying Hard to Preserve
Their Pricing Power," *Wall Street Journal*, September 24, 2019,
https://www.msn.com/en-us/money/companies/drugmakers
-are-lobbying-hard-to-preserve-their-pricing-power/ar
-AAHLDDg?li=BBnb7Kz.

"Deloitte 2017 Survey of US Health System CEOs," Deloitte,
https://www2.deloitte.com/us/en/pages/life-sciences-and
-health-care/articles/health-system-ceos.html.

"CMS Fast Facts," CMS.gov, https://www.cms.gov/Research
-Statistics-Data-and-Systems/Statistics-Trends-and-Reports
/CMS-Fast-Facts/index.html.

"Health Insurance Coverage of the Total Population,"
Kaiser Family Foundation, https://www.kff.org
/other/state-indicator/total-population/?current
Timeframe=0&sortModel=%7B%22colId%22:%22
Location%22,%22sort%22:%22asc%22%7D.

"Does Medicare Cover MRI Scans?," eHealth, https://
www.ehealthinsurance.com/medicare/coverage-all
/does-medicare-cover-mri-scans.

"History of Hospitals," Penn Nursing, https://www
.nursing.upenn.edu/nhhc/nurses-institutions-caring
/history-of-hospitals/.

"Hill-Burton Free and Reduced-Cost Health Care," Health Resources and Services Administration, https://www.hrsa.gov /get-health-care/affordable/hill-burton/index.html.

Luca Ventura, "World's Largest Companies 2019," *Global Finance*, August 29, 2019, https://www.gfmag.com /global-data/economic-data/largest-companies.

"2015–2016 SUSB Employment Change Data Tables," United States Census Bureau, https://www.census.gov/data /tables/2016/econ/susb/2016-susb-employment.html.

"Questioning the 80/20 Rule for Health Care," Deloitte, https://www2.deloitte.com/us/en/pages/life-sciences-and -health-care/articles/is-80-20-rule-of-health-care-still-true -population-value-based.html.

Liz Hamel et al., "The Burden of Medical Debt: Results from the Kaiser Family Foundation/New York Times Medical Bills Survey," Kaiser Family Foundation, January 5, 2016, https://www.kff.org/report-section /the-burden-of-medical-debt-introduction/.

"Economic Trends in Tobacco," Centers for Disease Control and Prevention, https://www.cdc.gov/tobacco/data_statistics /fact_sheets/economics/econ_facts/index.htm.

"Economic Costs of Diabetes in the U.S. in 2017," American Diabetes Association, https://care.diabetesjournals.org /content/early/2018/03/20/dci18-0007.

"Excessive Alcohol Use," Centers for Disease Control and Prevention, https://www.cdc.gov/chronicdisease/resources/publications/aag/alcohol.htm.

Buddy T., "The Dangers of Substance Abuse in the Workplace," *Very Well Mind*, July 6, 2019, https://www.verywellmind.com/substance-abuse-in-the-workplace-63807.

Joey Mattingly, "Understanding Drug Pricing," *U.S. Pharmacist*, June 20, 2012, https://www.uspharmacist.com/article/understanding-drug-pricing.

Makary, Marty. *The Price We Pay.* Bloomsbury Publishing, 2019.

TERMINOLOGY

Aggregate: Insurance that protects the group plan for claims that exceed a fixed level and appropriate for that size employee group.

Attachment point: The maximum dollars of claims that a group/company will have to pay for in a given plan year.

BUCA: Industry term for the nation PPO carriers Blue Cross, United Healthcare, Cigna, and Aetna.

Chargemaster: Price list that medical providers, doctors, hospitals have in order to file their insurance claims.

Co-Insurance: The amount of money a patient pays as part of the total payment paid to a medical provider. Normally this is a percentage of the total bill.

Co-Pay: The initial amount of money a patient pays to a medical provider for an appointment or procedure.

Cost shifting: Transferring cost from one party to another; in today's medical insurance environment, the shift in cost is from the company or plan sponsor to the employee or medical plan member.

Deductible: The amount of money a patient is responsible for before the insurance policy will pay on a medical claim.

Direct primary care: A membership payment system whereby individuals and families obtain primary medical care from a designated doctor. Normally a monthly service fee provides concierge level service with your doctor, more face time with your doctor, and little or no waiting time in the office.

Explanation of Benefits: a document from an insurance company or TPA giving specific information about the medical procedure, cost, and patient responsibility. This document also gives you information about the deductible amount met year to date.

Fully Insured: insurance program utilizing a PPO network, level monthly premium, and no additional risk or financial responsibility for the plan members, company, or plan sponsor.

Level-Funded: An introductory self-funded insurance program with a level monthly premium. Carriers have different programs but normally these types of plans only have an aggregate stop-loss feature. There is no limit on an individual's claims, just a maximum liability for total claims paid number for the group.

Maximum exposure: The maximum amount that the group, company, or plan sponsor must pay in a year for member claims. This is sometimes referred to as the attachment point.

Maximum Out of Pocket: The maximum amount an individual or family must pay during the plan year. This is the total patient responsibility that a member or their family is responsible to pay for all medical procedures.

Medical cost-share program: A membership program where members help each other pay their medical bills. Normally includes some form of monthly contribution, premium, or minimum payment. Medical bills are shared with the group, and individual members contribute any amount they choose until the total bill is paid. There is no network and no predetermined discount off the chargemasters.

Partially-Self-Funded: another term for a self-funded medical plan. Often used to help define a medical plan that includes a level of insurance to protect the plan and sponsor from catastrophic claims.

Spec Deductible: The plan deductible for an individual in a self-funded medical plan. This is the amount that the plan must pay before the insurance will pay for that individual.

Specific stop-loss: The insurance coverage that pays for claims on an individual for claims (medical bills) over the spec deductible.

Stop-loss insurance: The general term for the insurance that protects a self-funded medical plan.

Telemedicine: A new way to access primary medical care via a phone call or video chat. About 70 percent of what is diagnosed in an office visit can be diagnosed through telemedicine.

Third-party administrator: A company that pays medical claims for a self-funded medical plan. This company also provides customer service, ID cards, and a network to medical doctors, hospitals, and surgery centers.

Transplant: When a member needs a new organ, like a heart, kidney, or liver. This is a long and very expensive process. Many policies limit or exclude transplants due to the cost. A specific transplant policy covers the costs of this procedure.

Utilization: A global term for medical claims for a group. This represents how much a group of members uses their medical plan. This could be measured by the number of procedures completed or the total dollars of claims.

OTHER RESOURCES

Allied National
http://www.alliednational.com/

Cardiovascular Health Clinic
https://cvhealthclinic.com/
Dr. Dwayne A. Schmidt & Dr. Jim G. Melton

Evolution
http://myevolutionbenefits.com/

Free Market Medical Association
https://fmma.org/

MaxCare RX
https://www.maxcarerx.com/

Occunet
https://www.occunet.com/

Physicians ER
Dr. Christion Rice
https://mdpremier.com/

Resource One Administrators
    https://roatpa.com/

Self-Insured Institute Of America
    https://www.siia.org/i4a/pages/index.cfm?pageid=1

Society of Professional Benefit Administrators
    https://spbatpa.org/

Surgery Center of Oklahoma
    https://surgerycenterok.com/
    Dr. Keith Smith & Dr. Steven Lantier

Notes

Introduction

1. *Oxford English Dictionary*, s.v. "freedom," https://www
.lexico.com/en/definition/freedom.
2. "NHE Fact Sheet," CMS.gov, https://www.cms.gov
/research-statistics-data-and-systems/statistics-trends-and
-reports/nationalhealthexpenddata/nhe-fact-sheet.html.
3. "What's Medicare?," Medicare.gov, https://www
.medicare.gov/what-medicare-covers/your-medicare
-coverage-choices/whats-medicare.
4. "An Overview of Medicare," Kaiser Family Foundation,
February 13, 2019, https://www.kff.org/medicare/issue
-brief/an-overview-of-medicare/.
5. "Who Is Eligible for Medicaid?," HHS.gov, https://www
.hhs.gov/answers/medicare-and-medicaid/who-is-eligible
-for-medicaid/index.html.
6. "June 2019 Medicaid and CHIP Enrollment Data High-
lights," Medicaid.gov, https://www.medicaid.gov/medicaid
/program-information/medicaid-and-chip-enrollment
-data/report-highlights/index.html.
7. Katie Keith, "Two New Federal Surveys Show Stable
Uninsured Rate," Health Affairs, September 13, 2018,

https://www.healthaffairs.org/do/10.1377/hblog 20180913.896261/full/.

8. "CMS Fast Facts" CMS.gov, https://www.cms.gov /research-statistics-data-and-systems/statistics-trends-and -reports/cms-fast-facts/index.html.

9. "US and World Population Clock" United States Census, https://www.census.gov/popclock/.

10. "Health Insurance Coverage of the Total Population," Kaiser Family Foundation, https://www.kff.org /other/state-indicator/total-population/?current Timeframe=0&sortModel=%7B%22colId%22:%22 Location%22,%22sort%22:%22asc%22%7D.

Chapter 1: How Did We Get Here?

1. "Our History," Baylor, Scott, and White Health, http:// news.bswhealth.com/pages/history.

2. Alex Blumberg and Adam Davidson, "Accidents of History Created U.S. Health System," National Public Radio, October 22, 2009, https://www.npr.org/templates /story/tory.php?storyId=114045132.

Chapter 2: Show Me the Money

1. "Historical," CMS.gov, https://www.cms.gov/research -statistics-data-and-systems/statistics-trends-and-reports /nationalhealthexpenddata/nationalhealthaccountshistorical .html.

2. "The World's Largest Public Companies," *Forbes*, https:// www.forbes.com/global2000/list/#tab:overall.

3. "What Does One Million Dollars Look Like?," Page Tutor, https://www.pagetutor.com/trillion/calculations.html.

4. "Premiums for Employer-Sponsored Family Health Coverage Rise 5% to Average $19,616; Single Premiums Rise 3% to $6,896," Kaiser Family Foundation, October 3, 2018, https://www.kff.org/health-costs/press-release /employer-sponsored-family-coverage-premiums-rise -5-percent-in-2018/#.

5. "Premiums and Worker Contributions Among Workers Covered by Employer-Sponsored Coverage, 1999–2019," Kaiser Family Foundation, September 25, 2019, https:// www.kff.org/interactive/premiums-and-worker -contributions-among-workers-covered-by-employer -sponsored-coverage-1999-2018/#/?coverageGroup=family.

6. "Premiums for Employer-Sponsored Family Health Coverage." Kaiser Family Foundation, October 3, 2018, https://www.kff.org/health-costs/press-release/employer -sponsored-family-coverage-premiums-rise-5-percent -in-2018/.

7. "Facts and Data on Small Business and Entrepreneurship," Small Business and Entrepreneurship Council, http:// sbecouncil.org/about-us/facts-and-data/.

8. Dave Chase, "Have PPO Networks Perpetrated the Greatest Heist in American History?," *Forbes*, September 5, 2016, https://www.forbes.com/sites/davechase/2016/09/05 /have-ppo-networks-perpetrated-the-greatest-heist-in -american-history/#ea2515433300.

9. "The Role of the Hospital Chargemaster in Revenue Cycle Management," *Revcycle Intelligence*, February 9, 2018, https://revcycleintelligence.com/features /the-role-of-the-hospital-chargemaster-in-revenue -cycle-management.

Chapter 3: New Lenses, New Perspective

1. Gulfstream Specifications,
   https://www.gulfstream.com/en/aircraft#gulfstream-g600.
2. Cessna Specifications,
   https://www.cessnaflyer.org/specifications-105.html.
3. "How Do Health Expenditures Vary Across the
   Population?," Peterson-Kaiser Health System Tracker,
   https://www.healthsystemtracker.org/chart-collection
   /health-expenditures-vary-across-population/#item
   -discussion-of-health-spending-often-focus-on-averages
   -but-a-small-share-of-the-population-incurs-most-of-the
   -cost_2016.

Chapter 5: Personal Responsibility

1. Kimberly Amadeo, "Health Care Costs Facts,"
   Balance, June 25, 2019, https://www.thebalance.com
   /healthcare-costs-3306068.
2. Amadeo, "Health Care Costs Facts."
3. Wullianallur Raghupathi and Viju Raghupathi, "An
   Empirical Study of Chronic Diseases in the United States:
   A Visual Analytics Approach to Public Health," March
   15, 2018, https://www.ncbi.nlm.nih.gov/pmc/articles
   /PMC5876976/.
4. Timothy B. Norbeck, "Drivers of Health Care Costs,"
   Missouri Medicine (March–April 2013), https://www
   .ncbi.nlm.nih.gov/pmc/articles/PMC6179664/.
5. "Current Cigarette Smoking Among Adults in the United
   States," Centers for Disease Control and Prevention,
   https://www.cdc.gov/tobacco/data_statistics/fact_sheets
   /adult_data/cig_smoking/index.htm.

6. "Current Cigarette Smoking."

7. "Smokeless Tobacco Use in the United States," Centers for Disease Control and Prevention, https://www.cdc.gov/tobacco/data_statistics/fact_sheets/smokeless/use_us/index.htm.

8. Tanya Albert Henry, "Adult Obesity Rates Rise in Six States, Exceed 35% in Seven," American Medical Association, November 26, 2018, https://www.ama-assn.org/delivering-care/public-health/adult-obesity-rates-rise-6-states-exceed-35-7.

9. "Statistics About Diabetes," American Diabetes Association, https://www.diabetes.org/resources/statistics/statistics-about-diabetes.

10. "New CDC Report: More Than 100 Million Americans Have Diabetes or Prediabetes," Centers for Disease Control and Prevention, https://www.cdc.gov/media/releases/2017/p0718-diabetes-report.html.

11. "Alcohol Facts and Statistics," National Institute on Alcohol Abuse and Alcoholism, https://www.niaaa.nih.gov/alcohol-facts-and-statistics.

12. "Economic Trends in Tobacco," Centers for Disease Control and Prevention, https://www.cdc.gov/tobacco/data_statistics/fact_sheets/economics/econ_facts/index.htm.

13. "Obesity Drives U.S. Health Care Costs up by 29 Percent, Varies by State," Science Daily, February 8, 2018, https://www.sciencedaily.com/releases/2018/02/180208180356.htm.

14. "Economic Costs of Obesity," National League of Cities, https://www.healthycommunitieshealthyfuture.org/learn-the-facts/economic-costs-of-obesity/.

15. "The Costs of Obesity in the Workplace," National Center for Biotechnology Information, https://www.ncbi.nlm.nih.gov/pubmed/20881629.

16. "Economic Costs of Diabetes in the U.S. in 2017," American Diabetes Association, https://care.diabetesjournals.org/content/early/2018/03/20/dci18-0007.

17. "Excessive Alcohol Use," Centers for Disease Control and Prevention, https://www.cdc.gov/chronicdisease/resources/publications/aag/alcohol.htm. Most recent statistics are from a 2010 CDC report. This report estimates that the true cost of alcoholism is underestimated due to limited hospital reporting, lack of diagnosis, limits in workplace reporting, and limited reporting on the part that alcohol plays in illicit drug use or reporting.

Chapter 6: Protection

1. "Top 50 Global Reinsurance Groups," *Reinsurance News*, https://www.reinsurancene.ws/top-50-reinsurance-groups/.

Chapter 7: Choices

1. Jack Matthews, "U.S. Auto Sales Brand Rankings— September 2018 YTD," Good Car Bad Car, October 2, 2018, http://www.goodcarbadcar.net/2018/10/u-s-auto-sales-brand-rankings-september-2018-ytd/.

Chapter 8: Controls

1. "Why Do Insurance Companies Have Deductibles?," *Investopedia*, August 8, 2019, https://www.investopedia.com/ask/answers/071515/why-do-insurance-policies-have-deductibles.asp.

2. "275+ Telehealth Companies to Know—2019," Becker's Hospital Review, June 28, 2019, https://www .beckershospitalreview.com/lists/275-telehealth-companies -to-know-2019.html.

Chapter 9: Final Thoughts

1. "The Top Ten Pharmaceutical Companies by Market Share in 2018," Pharmaceutical Technology, March 7, 2019, https://www.pharmaceutical-technology.com /features/top-pharmaceutical-companies/.

About the Author

TROY REICHERT is the Chief Revenue Officer of Coral, LLC, a technology company helping employers, TPA's, and health-care providers streamline and manage their processes to reduce expenses and improve patient outcomes. In this role, he directs sales, marketing, and customer service to bring a creative, holistic, and global approach to employee benefits. He holds a BA degree from Wheaton College and an MBA from Vanderbilt University's Owen School of Management. Troy is a multiple-year recipient of the GAMA Leadership Award. An effective leader and public speaker, he has traveled around the country working with clients, developing creative solutions, and talking to groups about change management. Troy's passion for motivation, leadership, and education runs deep, extending well beyond work and career. He has been a volunteer with Junior Achievement teaching students about work readiness, entrepreneurship, and financial literacy and has also been an active coach in Little League and high school sports. He is an avid outdoorsman, photographer, and writer. Troy and his wife, Tami, have been married for more than thirty years and have a daughter, three sons, and one grandson.